W/Reckless Love

W/Reckless Love

Poems by

Robert Harlow

Cover design by Shay Culligan
Cover image by Todd Trapani on Unsplash

ISBN: 979-8-90146-810-4
Library of Congress Control Number: 2026931916

Kelsay Books
502 South 1040 East, A-119
American Fork, Utah 84003
Kelsaybooks.com

For my sisters—
Barbara Troxell & Bette Gold

Acknowledgments

Thank you to the following publications, in which versions of these poems previously appeared:

The Beatnik Cowboy: “After Language”
Chronogram: “Cartography,” “Overheard in a Bookstore,” “The Page,” “What Cannot Be Found”
Concision Poetry Journal: “Probably”
Foxtail: “Short Subjects”
Hudon Valley Writers Guild: “My Slender Book—The Loaner Version,” “Overheard in a Bookstore”
January Review: “Hearing What You Want to Hear”
Live Nude Poems: “Third Day’s Matins”
The Lyric: “The Hardest Part”
The Midwest Quarterly: “Guided Tour”
The Milk House: “Out in the Pasture,” “Still Falling Snow,” “*To Plant a Tree*”
Rat’s Ass Review: “Landscape: Woman in the Snow Without Dogs”
Raven’s Perch: “Something’s Between Us”
RHINO: “Looking for Petey: The Parakeet Expeditions”
San Antonio Review: “The Lost Among Us”
The Sandy River Review: “Do They or Don’t They”
Soul Poetry: “Birthday Kites,” “Different Orbits,” “Snow in Paris,” “Snowing Still,” “Tomorrow Maybe, Not Today”
Spindrift: “Companions”
Stone Canoe: “Mating for Life”
Talking River Review: “The Day Trout Fell from the Sky”

Contents

Still Falling Snow

The woods are mine now
and they fill up with snow
more often than I'd like.
The nearest farmhouse
fallen into itself,
helped these last few years
by a seasonal crush of snow
turned to ice deep on the roof,
breaking ridge-pole and rafters
hand-hewn almost two centuries ago.
Most nights, my pastured horses
return from the far fields
before I have to call them to the barn.
I don't know when they sleep
because they always seem to be awake
when I check on them sometime around midnight
after making my way home from work.
The roof over their heads will last
their lifetimes and far longer than mine.
I wonder if they are grateful for the miles
I have to travel to keep them here,
groomed and fed and seldom-ridden
through nearby long-abandoned and forgotten farms.
Field-stone foundations and stone fences
are all that define what used to be,
but they too are snow-erased now.
Every night I count the miles I have to travel
before I'm the one who gets to sleep.
The road home, the distance
through the dark snow, are what I have
to remember, claim as my own, the clarity

that becomes something easier to understand
when the lights in the yard guide me
up the last slow hill, making the barn rise
out of the still falling snow.

Preferential Treatment

> *Whereupon the conversation turned to the subject of women. Pellerin couldn't agree that there was such a thing as a lovely woman. He preferred tigers.*
>
> —Flaubert, *Sentimental Education*

It's not for me to decide how lovely they can be
when two of them sit beside me. They sit beside me
and whisper. They see me and come up and sit,

one on each side. Exchanging glances, one of them says,
"Touch me. Touch us." The other one, the quiet one,
closes her eyes in an act of devotion as if she were praying,

while her companion nuzzles my cheek and asks,
"Have you been sitting here very long?
Have you been wondering when we would arrive?

We didn't mean to keep you waiting."
As the quiet one starts purring close to my ear,
her not-so-coy friend says, "She likes you.

She has always liked you. I like you too.
Tell us your name. Tell us where you live
so we can go there too. But before that can happen,

there's something we need to know—
do you prefer women or tigers?"
Aren't they one and the same? I ask myself—

untamable, elusive, dangerous, even deadly at times.
Certainly, they have unpredictability in common.
Personal history tells me this,

but when have I ever listened to myself before?
And then the quiet one says, “Only the rest of your life
depends upon what you say now.”

Touch me, I say, because they are the only words I know
by heart now, having heard them somewhere before.
Exchanging glances again, they take me by my hands,

gently, almost shyly, and move ever so much closer
as we start walking toward what, I desperately need to believe,
will be our perfect home, parting the deviously fragrant air

that seems to be the only air left for us to breathe
now that the choice has been made when the subject
of women versus tigers comes into play.

The Day Trout Fell from the Sky

I was minding my own business
which mainly consisted of avoiding
any sort of flora, fauna, or marine life
coming at me with any velocity
from any distance or direction.
But *you can't always get what you want,*
Mick Jagger tells me every now and then,
so, when the headless rainbow trout
hit me on the head, I knew
that more than the sky was falling.
At first, I thought maybe an eagle
or osprey dropped it, although
I couldn't see one no matter where I looked.
If it did, then I have to commend its aim,
although I do have to question its motives.
If it didn't, then some sort of cosmic reversal
must be the newly revised, unannounced
order of the day, one in which I should cast my line
into the sky instead of the Flathead, the river
I was walking toward, dazed, confused, and contused.
A chowder-headed easterner shipwrecked
and adrift in Big Sky Montana. And it does seem
as if the sun is emerging from the water now
instead of sinking into it with an audible
scowl and hiss as it usually does this time of day,
making me question my place in the grand scheme
of things. "Why me?" I asked out loud,
but there was no one around to answer
or who witnessed the raining of this rainbow trout
in all its iridescent glory, no one to show

its trophy length, girth, and width—
even headless as it is—no one
to tell me whether or not it’s a keeper.

Mating for Life

In the sleep-long dawn,
star-shorn, thin-trimmed
clouds arc and arch,
lie slender, layer on layer,

somewhere where
they fall softly down,
falling beyond perception,
breathed out of being

before gathering again.
And then the warm
mute swan of her hand
lightly alights, soft as narrow

and as the sky is long,
nests into mine.
So easy to remember,
the sound, the touch like feathers,

the returning, even if
it's just from another room.
Like a migratory flight
where warmth can always be found

waiting upon arrival,
wings folding in rest.
The ones that allow us to fly.
The ones that keep us landing here.

New Golden Rules, 2021

Windows don’t have masks.
People inside them sometimes do.

People outside them are supposed to
but not everyone obeys.

Silly to think that a mask
lets others know where you stand—

I’m protecting myself, the ones
I love, and you as well.

That’s only fair, isn’t it?
At least it should be.

Groceries and paper goods.
Who knew we’d have to touch

the produce, and each other,
with latex gloves?

And stay six feet apart.
That’s probably a good rule

to follow most of the time anyway,
but I always give it up, going back

to the old ways, when coming home,
groceries in hand, taking off

gloves and mask and my clothes,
A superhero of sorts,

lying beside her with nothing
but the touch of her skin

touching mine, as close as we can get.
No rules here to get in the way.

Tomorrow Maybe, Not Today

Solace and sorrow.

You shouldn't ask me
about such words.

They are too new
to be of use.

Someone dies
but you don't.

What good are words
that are offered

when what is missing
takes the place

of everything else?
Sight and sound disappear

as if being deaf
and blind is an answer.

A way to live
through absence,

through solace,
through sorrow.

But not right now.
Maybe tomorrow.

Certainly not today.

Message in a Bottle

I like living on the edge of the continent
because of the options and adventures
here at home and abroad in Wellfleet.

And I like writing, call them poems
if you want. I don't call them that.
I don't call them anything

because I learned a long time ago that
they do not answer to any name I give them.
It seems they have a mind of their own.

And when they leave home
I like to think of them as messages
in bottles I throw into the sea,

hoping some of them will reach a near
or distant shore where they will wash up,
be found, opened, read, maybe even cherished.

And wondered about—but just a little—
because I'd like them to find a home
for a while before being passed on, traveling

for years, I hope. Living hand to mouth if need be.
And some, I want to believe, would just
continue sailing on, the bright, tropical sun

lasering off the glass, and that someone on shore,
or a passing ship, sees, but the bottle
always stays just beyond reach, always

just far enough away to make them wonder
just what it is they are missing,
and, Oh, so very near at hand.

My Slender Book—The Loaner Version

Occasionally, not purposefully,
I'll stop in the stacks and reach for it,
hoping it's not there, always dismayed
if it is, almost always stunned
when it isn't on loan, borrowed
and renewed time after time.
But if it is there, I take it down
from its rightful place right next to
any book of poems by Robert Hass,
where it has a good chance
of being discovered by proximity,
if not by reputation or word of mouth.

Standing beneath a rowdy fluorescent light
and the air conditioning pouncing
on my back, I let the book fall open
to whatever page it wants
and read just one page or poem
(sometimes more, or many more,
even though I know most of them
by heart) before putting the book back,
tidying the shelf, but making sure
it projects a bit beyond its neighbors
before moving on to find the book
I came for in the first place.

If my book is nowhere to be found,
you might notice a slight smile
on my face as I wait at the check-out desk,
trying to see the titles of the books
other patrons hold in their hands.

But I sometimes hope someone stole it,
after reading a few lines, because they wanted
to possess it all to themselves, still keeping it
even after misunderstanding a book entitled
Places Near And Far is a much different
guidebook than they've ever read before.

Tangled

Although I was there
   when it happened,
I don't remember it very well.

How they got there, that is—
   her dress, my shirt, my pants,
our shoes, all the rest.

Somehow they must have been
   dropped on the floor.
"We'll have to sort them out soon,

before we have to go back," I said.
   Not together, but to where we belonged.
"But not yet," she said. "Not yet."

Snowbound

It was almost as if she was cupping fire
in her hands when she touched me, weaving me
across the bed that accepted her sinuous grace,

unfolding, accelerating, blazing up, not all at once—
but almost—so that time didn't have a chance
to spiral to a stop but went on like an eclipse

of the sun and moon in the same place, at the same time,
in the same sky now being shouldered out of the way.
That's how disruptive that moment was that began

when she came up to my rooms to borrow a book,
talking through the afternoon, not paying attention
to what was going on outside, then realizing the snow

was coming hard and fast, relentless in fact.
We turned the radio on to hear the weather was dire.
The news told us the subway had shut down.

"I guess I'll have to stay," she said. And as it went on
in that unplanned, unexpected but welcomed
undergraduate afternoon, and the few days ahead,

surrounded by snow no one saw coming, we found out
what it means to forage our way into the unknown,
learning that the past was no longer a place

where we did not know each other
in ways we knew each other now,
no longer needing to bend

or break branches to mark a trail
    to help us find a way back
        now that we have found our way here.

The Lost Among Us

I don't know their names but I know their faces
and they're not here.

I'd like to think that what is true
cannot recede or be forgotten.
Like faces. Like names. Like the lost
among us. The disappeared. Stolen.
Beyond recovery. No longer recognized.
Or just dead and buried.
When the earthquake took away
most of a nearby village and part of hers,
the woman who survived told a reporter her story,
her search, digging for those who could not be found.
Among them two of her children.
Of course, it's not the same thing, that pain,
but, in a way, it's like a disease of the elderly
where names and faces disconnect
then cannot be recognized or recalled.
Nothing can make them come back.
They cannot be recovered from the debris
no matter how deep or long you dig.
It's as if you no longer have the ability
to understand why you are digging,
or know why and when you should stop,
until someone claiming to be your son
or daughter or spouse, or someone
who lives nearby, takes the shovel
from your hands. Someone whose face is there
but whose name is amongst the missing.

So you let them have the shovel
because it seems to be very important
to them now, but you don't know why.
Maybe they want you to rest for a while.
Maybe they just want to help you dig.

The Hardest Part

In another time, half-shadowed light
would be enough. Its fall through grace
like the slow descent of an untethered kite.
In another time, half-shadowed light
would continue its slow fall despite
not wanting to be seen, leaving no trace.
In another time half-shadowed light
would be too deep to fall back into grace.

Now comes the hard part—believing nothing
can replace what is lost. Like the look in her eyes
receding in time and memory. Like our slow dancing
before the harder part, before believing nothing,
not even how she looked, before she stopped believing
whatever I said, before knowing even these words are lies.
Now comes the hardest part—knowing nothing
can replace what is lost, especially that look in her eyes.

Spain

Beyond the door
the white air beckons.
The blue descends.

Dogs pant through the heat
that makes them seem
as if they are dancing.

I cannot imagine
how the orange trees feel,
yet they continue

to interrupt the conversation.
They speak about
what they will offer

when they press themselves
against the knives
displayed by the wind.

They speak about
how we all give up our shadows
when night's theater deepens

with or without sorrow,
taking away all the colors
that invent and caress us

before slowly letting go,
one at a time, erasing
everything that ever was

beyond the door
where the blue descends
and the white air beckons.

Landscape: Woman in the Snow Without Dogs

She used to have them.
They used to be nearby.
Now all she can do is stand
where they used to be
and bless the snow
surrounding her,
threatening to take her away.

Slowly. Intentionally.
Maybe that's what happened
to the dogs.
She is not just any woman.
She is not a widow
no matter who says she is.
She doesn't know why,

at this moment, she thinks about
the dentist who showed interest in her
by showing her his tattoos.
He pulled up his sleeve.
On his arm, a parade of teeth.
Not everyone understands,
he tells her. She wonders why

he doesn't understand why they should.
When she goes home,
if that's even possible without the dogs,
she will change dentists.
Yes, she'll be disloyal to him.
Ranger! she calls out. *Rusty! Time to go home!*

She is a woman standing in the snow
repeating names she knows have consequences,
obligations, agendas, places to be.
If she would just look behind her,
the dogs think, as they look at each other,
she could see us sitting here,
teeth as white as the snow,
happy to know we are wanted.

Looking for Petey: The Parakeet Expeditions

Searching for my 85-year-old neighbor's missing parakeet
in Tucson where parakeet escapees abound.

This is the famous evaporation of the species.
I have saved the negatives. In them you can see
the responses quite clearly, though, of course,
we do not blame you. Or a distance of birds.
Consider the naming or renaming of things.
Is it to make them exist or simply to deny silence?
Who among us can find the words to say,
"If only I could see blue and yellow amongst the leaves?"
When out of his cage, allowed to fly free,
he usually perched on the frame of her glasses,
and she told me she didn't blame her neighbors,
the Navajo sisters who left the screen door ajar
when they came for a visit, although they blamed themselves.
Almost blind, she could not see what Petey could see:
a seam of air, a pull of light, a new world to explore,
one without windows or doors, so he leapt to the unknown.
We do not blame you. Of course, it is said that, once again,
you were seen in the vicinity while we tried to determine
the flight pattern of fictional birds. Birds more beautiful
than blood, imperceptible birds, a flurry and swirl of birds.
We have heard the earth chanting, seen bright things
rising to the fragile air that surrounds us, but is anyone
to blame for what happened here?
We know the act of speaking is a dangerous one,
but we say this in all honesty, we do not blame you.
And speaking for myself—I always tell the truth
even if I have to make it up—I do not blame you.
No one is to blame, though it may not seem so at the time.

There are things one must learn to do for oneself,
while searching for the right thing to say,
truthful but considerate, to account for birds,
blue and yellow, neon and blameless, no longer lit
from within. Just something simply discarded,
like a small, brightly colored rag, down in a nearby street,
something that might have had a name once,
so far away now from wondering why
it can no longer hear it being called or to follow
the sound of it to find its way home.

What Cannot Be Found

Losing someone is like losing ______.
Fill in the blank on your own
because there is no comparison,
no simile or metaphor you can provide
for someone other than yourself.
Nothing comes close.

If it hasn't happened to you, then be grateful
you don't know what it's like.
If it has, then you know
exactly how to leave the blank empty.
The thought of loss is part of the loss,
so how do you prepare

for that which has no preparation,
for what you don't want or need,
and how do you give it a name?
Doing so would be giving it somewhere
to reside, and once it has an address,
then it becomes a place you have to pass

from time to time, streets you cannot avoid
taking to or from home. No detour
would be too far if one was available.
Maybe that's a useful metaphor.
First you learn there is no peace
in the kingdom now,

nowhere to abide like there was before.
Just traveling without maps,
nothing to point out the dangers ahead,
far more than the ones in the past.
That's as close as I can come to finding
any words, simile or metaphor, to tell you

what it is like. Like everyone else
who found it before, and, like them,
knowing, not just believing at the time,
or far in the distance,
There are no words to say,
and knowing maybe there never will be.

Learning My *A*’s and *B*’s in Order to See

As a teacher of the visually impaired,
my wife tries to teach me
some letters of the Braille alphabet
she embossed with her Braillewriter
on paper that has a nice feel and flow.
But my calloused and scarred
carpenter’s fingers can’t read any of them
even when she takes my hands in hers
and moves them across the page.
She thought it would be good for me to know
what she does in her job because she already knows
what I do in mine, especially when I come home
from the emergency room with stitches and bandages—
mostly on my hands—and asks, “What did you do this time?”
The assumption being that I, not the weaponed tools
I use, was mainly at fault. And she often reminds me
of the night when we spent hours in the E.R.
waiting for the ophthalmologist to arrive
to remove a sliver of wood from one of my eyes.
Fortunately, no real damage was done.
Since then she’s had the notion
that I should learn Braille. Just in case.
“I’m not getting anywhere,” I tell her.
“I can see that,” she says, then adds,
“This might take a while, so we better start
with something easier, something
I know you can read with your hands.”

Then she removes her clothes and places my hands
on her body. "Close your eyes," she says,
"and take all the time you need. Let's see
if you remember what you learned from before."
Tracing letters on her skin with my fingers,
her feel and flow so recognizable I'd know it anywhere,
but I know she likes me to pretend
I'm learning her body's alphabet for the very first time.
Even without looking, I know she's starting to smile
when I start to sing softly, eyes closed,
"*B* is for it's time to *begin.* And *A* is for *again.*"

More Than Just Apples

There she is in the kitchen
washing them, placing them
in a bowl she made
not too long ago
to hold, among other things,
at least apples today.

Washing them in the sink
that rests upon the cabinets
I made much longer ago,
it now seems as if
they are the only ones
we have ever known.

And here she comes
bearing apples, the first ones
from the trees we planted
so many years ago,
knowing I cannot refuse,
so I take one from the bowl,
her hands still wet from the washing.

"That's the one I would have chosen,"
she says, knowing
I will offer it to her,
also knowing I will say—
because I always do—
"but we can share it."
As if there could be
any other way.

Out in the Pasture

Steep, the way horses pray for anything
in light's slow fall out of grace,
as if darkness doesn't matter,
seeing in the dark, seeing through it as well.
And their travels, merely a dance,
ecstatic when young, regal when full-grown.
The memory persists in the body
if not in the mind. But it does not matter
as long as it can be recalled, as long as the dance
was performed even if only one time.
Whatever brings it into being
is something I am so grateful for,
something they'll show me
on occasion—but only if they want to—
unlike me, who dances for them
any and all the time no matter where
or when or whoever is looking.
Careless and carefree whichever side
of the pasture gate I find myself on,
even dancing for them as the sun goes down,
this beautiful four-legged audience watching
out of their own kind of light,
out of their own kind of grace.

The Return of Dracula

Gone to California without a passport, Dracula poses
as an artist and moves in with a family.
—The plot of the 1958 film, according to *Turner Classic Movies*

When we looked for him, we were surprised to find him gone.
Without a passport, we didn't think he could get very far,
so, imagine how stunned we were to learn he was settled in
with a lovely and sunny California family.
Knowing how even just the slightest touch
of daylight ruins his plans, we wondered why
he chose the west coast for his latest artistic venture,
posing as someone or something he wasn't born to be.
Of course, there had to be a blond and beautiful daughter,
a goofy, surf-crazed son, and a mom and dad
believing perfection exists beneath every thrusting,
luminous palm tree encircling their home.
Like most of us who call ourselves, who *believe*
we truly are artists, the wisest among us know
it's just a pose, one that can easily be seen through
just as Dracula can be seen through when facing a mirror.
And there's plenty of those around the house
where the family and the increasingly lovely daughter pose
before taking Drac out to meet her also oh-so-pretty friends,
introducing him as the artist who is staying with her family,
telling them of the quaint custom he has of kissing people
on both cheeks before kissing them—it must be
a European sort of thing—on the neck. So deeply and lovingly,
just like you'd expect any real con-artist would do, while saying
he wants to paint your portrait, only after the sun goes down,
of course, for some reason not yet all that clear, or,
at the very least, make you the subject of a poem using words
he's never written, or dared to say, to anyone until now.

The beginning ends

in the foolishly mislabeled dark,
when the room anoints itself
with more and more shadows
than it did in the past.
But the story will always stay the same, won't it?
You and me the first time,
the fierce walls echoing nothing
on their own, one voice or another
smudged against the door,
strewn objects that oddly don't look out of place,
the furniture not as contentious
or sentimental as it used to be,
but trustworthy all the same,
and still strong enough to embrace us
as we embrace, your brand-new-to-me
presence a welcome surprise,
so one or both of us become speechless,
lit candle altering what light there is
into what light we need
as we go on from here searching for,
then finding, a reason to never leave.

My Wife Says “Snakebit” in Tennessee

Far more casual than any human should be,
she holds up her hand, blood coiling down
her index finger, and says, before I can ask,
“Snakebit.” As if that could ease my imagining
only the worst possible outcome, reaffirming
my belief that nature is out to get us.
Before I can catapult out of my chair,
she tells me why—a big black snake,
not a rattler or copperhead, which she knows by heart
because she is my southern girl and spends her time
in the garden with a greater intensity, devotion,
awareness, passion, and trust than I believe possible.
“About four foot long, I think,” she says,
spreading her arms and hands as if showing me
the size of a fish she hooked but set free,
that no one else saw to verify. And then adds,
“I picked it up again after being bitten,
but closer to its head and brought it to the woods
so the dogs won’t kill it. I know you
would have done the same.” And back out
she goes to the garden, my expert snake charmer,
one who knows right from wrong
when snakes are involved. One any rural church
around here would be proud to have her give a sermon.
Dancing, barefoot, with acceptable abandon
while telling the tale about serpents, the ones
who do more than speak in tongues—indoors or out—
before coming home to me where we also speak
with tongues while doing a far different kind of dance
with much greater abandon than we’ve ever done before.

Probably

Am I the only one
who loves the taste of fire?
Glass on the tongue,

shards in the mouth?
It's almost like the taste
of wounded bracelets

or scolded rain sent through the mail
with no return address
so they have to find a new home

just like the rest of us
when something similar occurs.
Wondering if it's possible

to live without being excited
by the promise of new adventures
syruped with flames, the promise

of a bruising new cuisine?
Sparks, embers, slivers,
liquid curled on the tongue.

Maybe fire as the reason why,
at least for now, I've chosen
to be remembered like this.

Companions

I always take them with me,
my hands, when I go out for a walk,
and never forget to take them
to the seashore, sea mist shrouding
what is from what isn't.
The invention of water
no one dared cross centuries long ago
because maps warned of dire consequences
the longest distance from shore.
So, the sailors turned back
before the worst could happen.
But not me. I went out once
and didn't turn back.
Other shores weren't even a surprise.
My hands remember.
They were there too when we arrived.
No language sufficed, but that's when
my hands came into play.
Although they wanted to know
where the voices were coming from,
understanding that *Just in the distance*
is not an answer, but it will have to do
until another one comes along.
Reaching for what they want to believe
is really true, like shells that cross over
into the erotic, holding them up to my ear,
showing me what I cannot do without them.

Maybe the answer is, praise them.
Keep them warm.
Let them embrace each other.
Let them know they are not alone.

Please Don't

Write all my whispers down
—Theodore Roethke, "Her Words"

Because they're meant to be heard not seen,
please don't write all my whispers down.

Think of them arriving, a warm breath,
soft, slow, close to your ear.

Even though they're meant to be true forever,
there's a chance they won't stay that way,

just as they're not meant to break your heart
even though they might when you remember them.

Even if you know they're not really true, just pretend
these words, these whispers, everything that's promised,

and keep repeating them, but only to yourself.
Think of them as something to make you stay

a little while longer, but you can't and you won't,
so lean close just one more time

as if these words are all that truly matters,
as if your very life depends on hearing them,

as if I’m the only one who doesn’t yet know
where they will lead and why.

Lake Baskets and River Pottery

—An 18th-Century Japanese Wood-Block Print

The boatman carrying baskets and pottery to the shore
doesn't seem interested in what he sees around him,
just the task at hand, occasionally nodding
to other vendors as they head toward town.
Rowing with his wife to the market in the village square,
just beyond the shore, takes close to three hours
to cross the lake as they do once a week
almost every month of the year, an all-day journey overland,
choosing to live on the opposite shore of the town
where reeds are more plentiful for weaving his baskets
and clay his wife uses for her pottery
from the banks of the river that feeds the lake.
They are well-known for the useful and beautiful
and necessary objects they make.
And for breaking the tradition
where men make pottery and women weave baskets.
Their children help as well, but they are at home
with their grandmother and have this day off
to do only what they want as long as they add wood
to the kiln every few hours and check that the reeds
soaking in the large wooden tubs stay submerged
and remain pliant as they have to be for weaving.
It will be another good day for their parents
at the market, selling everything they brought.
Returning home in the evening,
guided by lanterns placed on the shore,
one on both sides of the inlet, and one each
in the front windows of their home.

They do not need more than they already have,
just the lights to guide them, children who will be asleep,
waking in the morning to see what their parents
have brought them—some blue ribbons for the girl,
maybe a kite for the boy. They will grow up
not going to school in the market town,
because it is too far away and they are learning
all they need to know by watching their parents' hands.
The boy not old enough yet to row the boat,
but he will one day, just like his father and grandfather,
learning how to steer at night, not needing stars or the moon,
even if they are everywhere in the sky to guide him,
because his children will light the lanterns, that blink,
dimly at first, then shine, beckoning him home.

Sheltering Where One Can

Shelter can be anything. Noun or verb.
Sometimes a few words or just one.

Although it has to represent something,
it doesn't always have to be a place,

but it should at least have that implied quality.
Somewhere to abide. Even if it's not home,

the memory of one will suffice.
If you are given the choice,

someone once told me,
choose metaphor over simile—

like and *as* are not as good as *is*.
It's better to be rather than seem to be.

Think of a simile as a home away from home
and metaphor as a true home. Shelter.

Noun or verb. Refuge. Something needed
and provided. After all, isn't it better to be

a rose than to be like one? I tell her that, hoping
she'll believe me, believe I thought it up,

hoping she doesn't find out how much
of a thief and liar I am, stealing from one home,

bringing it here from there to share
whatever refuge words provide—

at least until something better comes along
and shelters in place, making itself comfortable,

finding what seems to be a nearly perfect fit.
Something to write home about one of these days

even if it's just to say only roses are roses.
Everything else is something else.

Maybe it only seems this way.
And maybe only in poetry.

Birthday Kites

How could I have forgotten,
only remembered when reading a book
about kites around the world, my first one,
the one I couldn't get to fly.
Was I eight or nine? I don't remember
much more than running the field behind our house,
my mother's encouragement not enough,
so, she took the kite in one hand,
the ball of string in the other,
kicking her shoes off, cotton summer dress
slightly above her knees as she ran, always faster
than her brothers and most of the neighborhood boys,
and up it rose, first rocking back and forth, then sailing
on its climb the length of string she played out.
Running to catch up, I heard her call,
There it goes! Come hold the string!
Even young as I was, I suddenly saw her
as she must have been as a young girl,
one of fourteen children in a Great Depression world,
every penny precious, but ten cents bought a kite,
her first one, the one she remembered most,
her father giving her the coin on her birthday.
At its highest point, the end of three-hundred-foot length,
she said she let the string go and watched the kite rise
to see how high it could fly, the string
tree-tangled in a hillside orchard two fields away.
The wind held it up all afternoon and evening.
Gone in the morning, she couldn't find it.

It was made to fly, wasn't it? she told me,
so, I let it go. My birthday gift to the kite.
When the price rose to twenty-five cents,
kites were too expensive to let go.
And I remember the heavy, shiny silver dollar
she gave me for mine that birthday morning.
So, what do you think? she asked.
Seeing my smile, she knew the answer—
an apple falling close, not far from the tree.

Do They or Don't They?

People Also Ask: "Do poets make a lot of money?"
—www.shmoop.com>careers>salary

First things first: poets generally don't make any money.
By "make," I think shmoop.com means *earn,*
and from my experience, no poet I know has ever earned anything
from writing poems. Except obscurity, that is.
Enough to last their lifetime and beyond.

A fair amount of people who do this just do it to do it,
as in there must be some joy to doing it in and of itself.
Sounds about right to me since none of my friends
seem to be interested in reading it. Or maybe
just not my poems. I'll have to ask.
There's also a pretty good beat going there—
just do it to do it . . . do it to do it . . . do it to do it.
But I might need a bit of clarification
about the words *do* and *it* to see if I'm on the right track.

They're not really in it to make cash.
Pretty much sums up what has happened to me
in whatever job I've ever had.
Cash is just another four-letter word I try not to use,
just like cash itself. If you don't have it,
you can't use it, and it can't use you.
Once I got a two-dollar check from a little magazine
that published one of my poems.
After cashing it I bought a cup of coffee.

You'll see these folks all over town hogging open mics
because that's what poets do, don't they?
Yes, our town is over-the-rim brim-filled with poets
and open mics, so many of each that they don't have to share—
just like the cash they don't have
and wouldn't share even if they did.

And shmoop.com tells me these rapscallions
spend more time sipping coffee
than actually writing any stanzas.
Well, you've got to stay awake somehow
if you want to grab and hog a microphone
to spew out a few unearned stanzas
you appropriated from an open mic event
the week before from the guy with the beard
(which proves he is a poet) who wouldn't stake you
to a cup of coffee even if he could afford one
or share his free refill. *Refills,* to be precise.
I would have bought some other poet a cup
if asked, but the ones I know are usually busy
at home, not writing verses, practicing nonchalance
at the mic, primping, and honing their continuous quest
of rising to obscurity, rarely if ever without pause
on the way there, alone or in pairs.

That's poets for you—shysters and shamans,
bedraggled, bearded (mostly the men, that is)
caffeine-pumped knuckle-walkers, pawing
the finally relinquished mic at the open mic,
breadless bread-winners who can only do
what they can do when they do it to do it,
do it to do it. (I think there's an echo in here.)
And sometimes some of them do it well.
Why don't you stop by some evening?

You don't have anything to lose, do you,
and drop some money into the hat
that's being passed your way.
Poets have to earn a living somehow,
don't they, shmoop.com, don't they?

Six Foot Two, Eyes of Blue

Tall as me,
she was a whirling dervish
in a lightning storm
striking the tallest object
in the landscape, which turned out
to be me, left sizzling, smoke
of that electrically discharged fire
steaming up from my clothes—
what's left of them—tattered,
fractured rags no longer resembling
what I was wearing
when I left the house to meet her,
not knowing of the explosions,
eruptions, cascading lava
she had in store for me,
my eyes spiraling a message,
not quite an S.O.S. but maybe
just a call for witness, not seeking
or requiring rescue, just a little
resuscitation afterwards, if needed,
mouth-to-mouth by her, preferably,
although the flames might be rekindled,
which isn't really a bad thing.
And if this singed, shredded,
spasming, spaghetti-entangled
brain can return to the launching pad
mostly, or even somewhat, intact,
then whatever I can remember
about it will be worth
the welcomed disability to ever see
the world the same way again,

and well-worth the cost of admission
to her unabridged autobiography,
the first three volumes leather-bound,
indexed, about to be translated
into who knows how many languages
we have here on this well-worn planet,
and destined never to go out of print.

After Language

After language
    discovered me
    I thought, Oh, oh,
I'm in for it now.

After language
    discovered me
    whispering, it said,
you can raise your voice now.

After language
    discovered me
    it said, who said
you could talk now?

After language
    discovered it could
    confuse me like this,
now it will not leave me alone.

Good Night, Paris Time

I heard her singing before I saw her.
Three a.m. on some *Rue De* something
in, of course, Paris, because where else
could this story have taken place?
Don't ask me which street or avenue
or boulevard, because I hadn't found
the guidebook map by then,
but was close enough to the *pension*
(is that the right word?)

where I had left my luggage
a few streets away, out and about
because I had just arrived that evening
and was still on Eastern Standard Time.
Coming from behind me,
a not-at-all shy voice singing "Michelle."
Then she passed me, riding a bicycle barefoot,
holding her shoes in the hand she was using
to steer, her other resting on her hip.

"Nonchalant," I thought as she passed,
singing the words the whole world was singing
that summer when The Beatles owned the world,
even Paris, where I suddenly found myself singing along.

Then she called out, *Bonsoir et Bonjour!*
as she circled back when I answered.
And yes, it was a very good evening
that led to a very good day, and a few more,
in, where else, of course, but Paris?

Third Day's Matins

Looking at her, wearing nothing
but morning's slow light,
one hand on the railing of the hotel balcony,
the other held above her eyes to shade them
from the deeply piercing sun,
he thought, I will never not remember this,
knowing she would turn to him, small smile
on her face, not say a word as she crossed
the tile floor, then kneel at the side of the bed,
reach for his hand then press it to her lips,
eyes rising to his. No matter what happens now,
or next, or whatever days that will follow,
he knew the sight of her at that moment
would always define what he wanted,
something that had no life of its own
without both of them, even though he knew
it had to, was going to end a few hours later,
and she would not have to say, because he knew,
He will be home this afternoon.
That would be it, wouldn't it? he thought,
wondering how do days like this end,
when you know from the beginning there will be
no way to erase them and no reason
why you should, even when someone says,
this cannot happen again, can it?

And will be said again,
maybe next time as a promise,
neither of them will believe, not as a question,
the few hours still open for everything,
for anything that needs to happen next.
And for morning prayers to be answered.

Snow in Paris

Because some people are sleeping,
it is snowing in Paris.
You can see it falling,
see it pause on a railing

bordering the best houses
on a boulevard nearby.

Put your hand out—
it will rest there too.
So soft, its touch, so soft
a memory when you write

then mail a letter
to tell her what Paris is like

and will always remain
in the snow without her.
Snow on a railing,
snow in the hand.

Some things can only be said
from a great distance.

Days pass, the snow gone,
the letter received, opened, read.
That distance held in her hands—
the ones you miss—promising a return.

One Promise I Kept

The what could never-be-otherwise
divinely articulated form

of the horse
gives in to a desire

to move closer to the fence
where I stand

under a summer-full tree
whose name I cannot remember

offering from my hand
quarter-sliced apples

and a few carrots
I promised to bring with me

the next time
I passed this way

To Plant a Tree

A PBS documentary

for W.S. Merwin

Mostly palm trees, native
to the island of Maui, where he lives,
but now he can no longer remember

their botanical or familiar names.
They are in a book somewhere,
written by an expert who visited once.

Losing sight of the visible world
means having to enter the one
made of touch, sound, scent,

so, hands have more meaning now
just as voices do. Still speaking
lines of poems he can no longer see

but cannot forget. Almost as if
he knows what this world will be
without him, celebrating each tree

placed with such care, he says,
If I could, I would plant a tree
on the last day of my life.

Beneath a Moon of Many Names

for Richard Shelton

Sonora Desert, 1982. New York, 2020

We sat under a slightly bruised moon
that was turning the tides of our blood
cold in December. *The Snow Moon,*
you told us, giving some other names as well—
Little Spirit Moon, Long Night Moon,
Moon When Deer Shed Their Antlers.
I don't remember the other names, so many of them.
Who knew that all these years later
I would find these names I wrote down that night
in a small notebook I carried in a back pocket.
Driving miles from Tucson, then walking out
into the night to celebrate the nearing end of the year.
I don't remember how many of us there were,
and can only recall a few of their names now,
as we found a place to sit to read our poems,
none of them, except yours, about the moon.
I do remember thinking the only way snow
could fall here in the desert southwest
was if it fell out of the moon, being surprised
a few days later when I walked across campus
under fat flakes that almost looked as confused
as me as they landed, disappearing without a trace.
And that night, as the desert paused around us,
we struggled to read under the almost-full moon
that didn't give enough light so we had to pass
a barely reliable flashlight hand-to-hand.

When it was your turn to read, the flashlight turned off.
Holding it close to your face, suddenly it burst into light.
Like getting hit in the face by the moon when clouds open,
you said. Then you read to us, to the antlerless deer—
even though there were none around—to the long night,
and to the little spirits which are always around,
of all the ways the moon had spoken to you
and taught you how to listen, even when
it was so coyly unwilling to give up its snow.

Talking to Myself

I don't need to know anything more
about her. Everything else, I'll invent,
so, this will have to suffice
if nothing else about her comes true,

as when you find yourself
some blue morning, shadows
just opening, merely hinting
about how they'll spend the day,

lengthening because of the light
that strikes familiar objects first
then the not so familiar
in this wounded morning

that tries not to repeat itself
like all the days before.
Yes, that's all I need
to make her fit into these words.

And even if I don't tell her
about them, even if she never reads
or hears them, she'll recognize herself
when someone who knows her

tells her what I said,
how it could never be anyone else.
But what I know, that she doesn't,
is how much better off she is without me.

But I can't tell her that,
for the obvious reasons,
at least not in this way
and not in words such as these.

If Only

Quiet, the hostess will find herself standing a long time
on the patio alone . . .

—Laura Kasischke, "Hostess"

If this happens again
I'm going to have to do something about it—
seeing what I think I'm seeing
that turns out to be something else,
confusing one word for another.
I guess I'll have to make an appointment
to get my eyes checked.
Why, I wondered, would the hostess
be standing on a *piano?*
Not that there's anything strange about that.
The oddest part is why she'd do so
alone and so quietly and for so long.
I'd stand there too, and would have,
alone, or with her, but I wasn't there,
wasn't invited. I know she knows
I could teach her a few chords
and melodies to make her feel less alone,
provide harmony as accompaniment
to the silence lacing its fingers all around her.
But first she'd have to step down
from the piano. And I would have given her
my hand but was by myself somewhere else
at the time, unlike all the guests on the patio,
looking in at her standing there, elevated,
not looking their way, some among them
wondering if someone should go in
and offer her something,

or to help her down, asking each other,
Isn't there someone else who can play the piano?
since the one who wasn't invited
clearly won't be arriving anytime soon.
They'd all like to dance or sing some songs
because it's getting to be uncomfortably quiet
on the patio, just like it seems to be on the piano.
At least that's what it would look like to me,
if only I were there. If only I had been invited
maybe I could have helped her find herself.
Few of us wants to be lost and alone for long.
Perhaps an occasional hostess does,
but I'm willing to bet this one really doesn't.
I'll let you know next time, if there is one,
and only if I'm invited.
Patios and pianos.
Who would have thought
they'd have so much in common?

Jack Lord Says, *Aloha!*

So this is what the original Steve McGarrett
of *Hawaii 5-O* chose to say, after not uttering a word
for more than a year, as I was told by his social worker,
a friend who asked if I wanted to meet Jack Lord.
Did he mean *Hello* or *Goodbye* when he said it
as he let me out his door after my short visit?
Or was he saying what it really means—
love, affection, peace, compassion, mercy—
leaving me to choose one or all of them.
Not a native Hawaiian, he lived there
long enough to know what things mean,
that a mainland *haole* might never know.
Did he know *aloha* also means
the force that holds existence together?
I'm sure he did and also sure
he wanted me to discover on my own
what comes true only after a long settling in
to a place that still treasures what is
always present, never hidden. But now
he has entered that tunnel from which
no one returns, where language erodes
bit by bit, faces cannot be recalled,
names just strange sounding syllables.
But he didn't look as if he was marooned there,
alone, life lived all internally, no longer speaking.
His wife, his only voice now, always by his side
to steer him from shore to shore within
their apartment overlooking a bay, a view
only a retired television star could afford,

the place he never leaves now that the world
has lost him and almost all meaning. *Aloha.*
Go find it is what I think he was telling me.
Where to begin, I asked myself, if not here,
as I turned to see Jack Lord on his balcony
waving hello and goodbye to me,
to someone who met him only once.
Just another name and face not to remember.
Just someone waving back, thinking, not speaking, *Aloha.*

Disturbances on the horizon

appear so quickly
they might be missed
unless you have some way

to make them stay put
until they can be examined,
rearranged if need be.

Simple matters of fact
of what is seen,
or what appears to be,

make you question
what might or might not be true.
But it's never inappropriate

to question what you see,
especially in these uncertain times.
Complacency

might be the worst thing
to have when what we believe
to be light strikes its bold shadows

on the far edges of what is seen.
Where *this* doesn't always follow *that,*
unusual as that may seem.

But only from a distance,
such as this one. Maybe
just a hand pointing,

or waving toward *there.*
Another hand waving back.
It just can’t be otherwise, can it?

Events Toward Evening

Everywhere the sound of pines,
even here where there are so few of them.
Their small, narrow leaves
lift in the air that shines with birds
while water kneels
at the foot of the moon
like pearls in a darkened hand.

In this blue, the bottom of the sky
is worn smooth against the pines,
against the receding light.
Birds whisper in the branches
while somewhere the earth leans
into the sun's mouth as the shallows
begin feeding owls to the moon.

I Like It Here

I like it here
where you can't ask the weather about itself.
You can only discuss it with each other
in chance meetings, maybe standing
at the end of a wayward sea-bound pier,
under a deeply blooded sun
intentionally arcing westward overhead,
the distant sky revolving swiftly
with billowed clouds and beneath it
the landscape throbs open
in its inevitable, enviable, mutable,
seasonably predictable way.
You can see it day by day, week by week,
month after month, year after year.
So much change.
Go to bed, pull up the shades
in the morning and there it is—
something new in the trees,
out in the street, on the lawn,
in the garden where the wind barters itself
for something breathtakingly open
or brazenly closed—the sky, snow, rain,
sleet, hail, and whatever else there is,
sometimes all the above, coming from above
until it stalls, sometimes for weeks,
where we dwell, and mostly behave,
as citizens participating in the world,
as if such things are natural here
where we have to belong
because it's where we truly belong,

looking at them, touching them,
talking about them, like anything
we need to make real, welcoming,
blessing whatever arrives
in order to make it our own.

Winter Chores

So much new snow.
Where did it come from

while I was sleeping?
All on different branches,

crows, cardinals, and blue jays
deeply whiten the snow.

What are they waiting for?
Oh, yes, I remember—yesterday

I forgot to fill the feeders
but will have to wait

until the snow stops falling
before clearing a path.

So deep it will take a while.
I can see that from here.

The Voice in Her Hands

Sometimes my heart breathes
slowly when she looks my way
as she combs her hair,

as she says my name,
snowfall echoing it too.
Not sometimes—always.

I like to hear her
say other things afterwards,
softly as the snow

when it falls at night,
when she puts her comb down,
then touches my hands,

silently, deeply,
as I listen to her hands,
that voice, call my name.

Instruction Manual

It doesn't matter what the scenery says,
or whether it lingers long enough for us to catch up,
    just hold me.

Or when the CD chatters and stutters up during the best part
of the song we slow dance to around the living room,
furniture destined to desert us still in place,
on some moon-laden night,
    hold me.

And when those raucous crows bebop below the feeder
and what they believe to be the campground I made,
and seem to be employed by, just for them,
    hold me.

Before and after the sun and moon change places,
a logical if clandestine meeting that concludes
the clockwork between them already firmly in place,
a treaty providing equal time and ample space
for what they need to do,
    hold me.

When I feel the need to get Norwegian,
my name Olaf, squinting during the sun's half of the day,
out over my picturesque village, fish-filled beyond possibility,
and you a glistening maiden with far more than just your eyes
fire-stoked, walking right out of the sun toward me,
    hold me.

And when the bract part of our house plants
disappoints our expectations—legendary
all by themselves—by deliberately not being
as “highly colored” as the seed package promised,
  hold me.

When I waken in the smallest cabin of the sloop I stole
a recently long time ago, hoping to fill a deep absence
in my navigable soul, painting your name over the name
on the transom, getting away with it so far, or so it seems,
  hold me.

And when the chronicle of this day or that one becomes illegible,
I wander motionless around the canticle of our home
so as not to disturb our most-of-the-time motionless cats
while waiting for you to come here and
  hold me

just like this, just like that, because I want you to, just like
I will do to you because I want to, and because you want me to,
and just to hear it said, even though no more words
need to show up now,
  “Hold me. Just hold me.”

Emily Shelters in Place

In Amherst when someone leans out of a car window
and asks the way to Emily's grave, one does not ask, "Emily who?"
—Robert Francis, *Pot Shots at Poetry*

Of course, you know which Emily I mean.
She was the queen of shelter in place,
being at home most of the time anyway.
In fact, she practically invented it.
Dressed in white, rarely seen from the street below,
maybe she was just waiting to be called,
mistakenly believed to be a health-care provider
or lab tech or at least a baker.
We all have to eat during a pandemic, don't we?
And she was famous for the goods she baked,
at least within her family, so she did provide
something of consequence even if
other members of her family weren't quite sure
about what she was doing, alone,
upstairs in her bedroom most of the time.
Young women behind closed bedroom doors.
The possibilities are endless in a way,
but in Emily's case there was only one:
make tiny, little poems, tie them neatly
into packets, giving one or two away.
Think of what the world would be like
if she had not done what she did.
While anything is possible, I don't believe
we'd be able to do what she did
no matter how long we sheltered in place.
Think of what came out of her self-exile,
as I so often do, remembering to thank her

for being a voyager, writing her letters to the world,
sacrificing nothing of value, needing nothing
beyond what she already possessed
in order to provide the words that act as vaccine,
words she needed to help her, and us, survive.

Overheard in a Bookstore

Standing nearby, I couldn't see the book's title,
but would like to believe it was mine.

"It's not fair," she said to her friend.
"All these words should be available

to everyone, not just poets."
I was hoping she wouldn't,

but then she put the book of poems back
on the shelf and they walked away.

Hoping now it was not mine,
but still disappointed in her decision,

I almost called out, "Wait. They are,"
but didn't want to tell them the truth—they aren't.

They're only available to the lucky few.
And only in the rarest of times.

Guided Tour

Tonight, I'm homeless
as the wind,
not to mention the snow—
that cruel white
that erases almost everything.

And when I hear someone say,
"Light. I've seen it
leaping from the earth,"
I do not know if I should run
to find a phone to call for help

or for information about the weather.
I'm sure the sentries at every border
consult my autobiography
and look at my picture hourly.
Though innocent, if they take me

to a little room, questioning me
relentlessly under deeply savage lights
for days on end, I will sign the confession
I always carry with me, the one
I have revised for years on a daily basis.

And if they want to add anything new,
even if they have to make things up,
just as I have always done,
I will beg them to include it.

I am not humble
when it comes to guilt or pain.
Consider this map I am holding:
is it my imagination,
or do roads lead nowhere
and go off the edges into oceans?

Just Because I Still Live Here

And because she is deep in the southern hemisphere,
in a country where it seldom if ever snows,
and I'm trying to balance being in the northern one,
where the opposite is true, at least here
where she used to live, I write to tell her it is snowing,
so it must be winter and someone has to live here.
That turns out to be me and so many other fools
who have to rationalize why we still remain,
pretending we have no other choice.

Me because she needed to place a new-for-her continent
between us, choosing a country where it's never cold,
where Portuguese is spoken so eloquently and properly,
especially when the sun barely slows down
its heat for the evening and palm trees whisper
as they weave shadows of their own making.
Now she reclines like she used to,
when there was no continental drift between us,
lightly clothed because it's always summer for her,

writing back to say, *I no longer do winter,*
adding a few other reasons as well.
Unlike her, stuck here, and stuck in just one language,
my only choice now is whether to clear the snow
off the driveway or the front walk first,
hoping I'm not the only one who remembers
what it costs to live here, as well as the deeper cost
of moving so very far away, knowing how easy it is
to be misunderstood no matter which language is spoken.

Hearing What You Want to Hear

I misheard the poet reading Rilke's
famous line, "You must change your life,"
from "Archaic Torso of Apollo."

Poor me, I've read it often enough
to know the reader didn't get it wrong
but thought I heard him say,

"You must change your *wife.*"
And she was sitting by my side
when he looked up from the page

and right at me, or so it seemed,
so I was almost certain
he said what I thought he said,

reading my mind from a short distance away.
A few months earlier she said,
"You can do anything you want with me,"

an offer I understood then
on a whole different level
than I took it to mean now,

backed up by the revised Rilke line.
When I walked away, did she understand
I was taking her up on her offer?

Whenever He Found Himself

In the near or far distance,
he always paused to remember the fragrant
and delinquent but always shallow fields,
basking in some sort of glow,
that he used to call home,
that he used as referent points,
before he gave in to the need
to be wanted wherever he found himself
attached to a landscape bursting with trees.
Limbs too far up to reach, to climb,
to fold over, so he had to find other uses
for them. So he gave them names
such as *useless,* and *cold.*
They chose *indifference* as a way to be
in his hands even as he embraced them,
thinking, "Who put all this ice here?"
Blue and serene, a village
no roads lead to or away from,
so isolate it never learned the words
lovely, lonely, but they are as intertwined
as the branches overhead, knitted and knotted,
so far from home, the place he needs
to touch in order to be recalled,
in order not to be forgotten.
A slight change of light now
could cause him to miss even the defining edges
of what he needs, so he has to be careful

about where he steps, walking backwards
so slowly, to make each footprint fit perfectly
into the ones he made on his way
to this place so that others who find them
will believe only one person passed this way.
One who was here. One who has gone.
One who never came back.

Cartography

I like to think of the poem
between us as a road,
not straight on to the horizon

and what is beyond
but so curved in its distance
there are too many bends

to see around.
Your only choice,
and the best one,

is to throw your maps away
and slow down
so you won't miss

all the enchanting sights
you can invent then visit
along the way.

Short Subjects

Revisions for Your Face

Liquid dogs settle down
in that place
where your eyebrows
growing together
burn like a signal fire
on the canyon's northern rim.

F.Y.I.

Pointing to the beard across the room,
she said, "He's a language poet."

I said, "Isn't all poetry language poetry?"
If not, I must be doing it wrong.

At Home with the Neighbors

Joining hands, we gather in a circle
to see who can hold out the longest
before making a break
for their lawnmower.

The Weather in Iowa City

"It snowed in Kansas today,"
my wife said after coming home
from work. "Well, baby," I said,

pulling her underpants down,
"this isn't Kansas,
and it ain't snowing here."

Music Lessons

A piano grows hungry.

I am afraid to go near it
because it wants my hands.

Australia

Sometimes
I sleep at the foot of the bed—

deliberately.

Something's Between Us

When I email to tell her it's snowing,
and about what I'm seeing now

out the window near where I'm seated,
she writes back to say,

How could a person resist the sight
of a porcupine in a tree?

Just one of the many things she's asked
that I don't have an answer for

now that she's no longer here
to see what I can see more clearly,

now that there's more than just distance
between us, now that she's on one coast

and I'm on the other, colder one,
now that there's just words between us

instead of something we once believed
as a promise never meant to be broken,

like something high up in the branches—
something untamable, forever wild.

This and That

This blush of skin,
this glistening wet-rose glow
that arises under touch,

long awaited,
counts for something.
If nothing else,

then a beginning. Again.
Add a slow slide of light
into the room

under the partially raised shade,
the open window,
and three crows squabbling

out on the lawn
at something or nothing
or just at each other,

obeying gravity
until they leap to the sky
when she closes the window

then pulls the shade
the rest of the way down,
before returning to that touch,

that soon-to-arise slow blush
when something nothing like
dew-wet rose petals open.

Wooly Bears

I don't know what's become of me
when I stop the car, get out, pick them up,
and usher them off the pavement.
Curled into a circle, not rolled
into a ball because they won't roll—
believe me, experience tells me that—
but lie flat, head to tail, or vice versa,
because it's hard to figure out
which end is which when they seek
the shelter of themselves,
dark brown and striped black,
or the other way around.
Swerving to avoid running them over,
exiting my vehicle when it's not always safe
to do so because it almost always happens
when there's a lot of traffic behind me
with highly precise and finely tuned horns
either praising me for what I'm doing
or giving me some other form
of friendly and encouraging advice.
Look at them waving at me!
I think that's what they're doing,
especially the guy a few cars back
telling me I'm *Number One!*
or at least I think that's what he means.
Only these little critters' safety—
not mine as much, for some reason—
matters because they contribute
more of what is needed to our world
than I probably ever will, pollinating

their way through life once they become
Tiger Moths, posing in their colors,
brightening their surroundings,
hiding their hindwings under
"cryptic" forewings, offering
an inedible target for predators.
Oh, to go through life like that,
knowing no one wants to eat you
and helping those who need pollen
to survive. And *cryptic forewings*—
you have to admit it would be nice
to have some of those.

The Page

Alone on the desk,
it casts its own light.

There is no sorrow there
or pleasure yet. It has to wait

for you to decide between the two,
inscribing one or the other

as a way to begin,
or so it lets you believe, anyway.

No, it just lies there
and will still be the same

no matter what words
rest on its body.

There will always be
enough blank space left over,

just as it knew there would be,
but you didn't because you can't

tell the difference yet
between telling the truth

or making something up.
Not that it matters

as long as someone like you
believes in it too.

Different Orbits

Whirling and twirling.
Is there any difference,
and does it matter?
I only ask this because
that's what I'm doing
in the backyard
so the neighbors won't have
any more fuel for the fire
that keeps me foremost in their minds
when they see me outside
for any length of time.
By default, because no one else
seems to want to be,
and because of self-selection on my part,
I'm the wacky neighbor.
But I can always be counted on
to lend a hand or tools when needed.
They know things about me
that are better left unsaid.
But this whirling thing
belongs only to me, spinning
while the trees stay in place,
reference points that might need
unscrambling once I fall down,
prone in body, still whirling along
at top speed in my mind.

If only they could see me now,
the neighbors, tethered to their laptops,
face-booking every moment of their lives,
while just over yonder I'm living mine,
planning, next time, to do this in the front yard
so whoever they're texting will believe
whatever is said about me,
one keystroke at a time.

Snowing Still

This too is geography,
another moment of it,
although the snow obscures
most of the distinguishing features,
fabricating something new.
Landmarks erased and replaced
slowly as snow changes
from nearly vertical to horizontal
right into your eyes,
so it's easy to lose your way.
Which isn't necessarily a bad thing,
unless you are growing concerned
about finding your way home,
about those who wondered
why you'd go into the woods
knowing where and when
it would fall into this mutable world
now lit only by snow
incapable of erasing the darkness
but capable of silencing any and every name
someone might call out—
if only from somewhere they would.

Notes

"The Day Trout Fell from the Sky" is based on hearing the gardener for the late James Welch's widow was hit on the head by a headless trout. He survived.

The quotation used as an epigraph for "The Lost Among Us" comes from a broadcast news report. I didn't make note of the source, date, etc., only the quoted verbatim statement from the woman being interviewed.

"Looking for Petey: The Parakeet Expeditions" is based on a fruitless search for my 85-year-old neighbor's parakeet in Tucson, Arizona, where parakeet escapees abound. She kept saying, "I don't blame them" in her despair over the sisters leaving her screen door slightly open when they came for a visit.

"Lake Baskets and River Pottery" is not based on a real 18th-century wood-block print. It is one I imagined.

The epigraph and italicized lines / statements in "Do They or Don't They" actually exist and can be found at the website noted in the poem. Surprising how accurate the answers to the question posed are.

"Jack Lord Says, *Aloha!*" is based on a social worker friend's comment that Jack Lord hadn't spoken a word for more than a year until he said Aloha to me.

"*The Return of Dracula*" is also the title of an actual film, and the brief description of the plot is a verbatim quote from the *Turner Classic Movie* channel. I didn't watch the film so have no idea if the plot of the film and the poem coincide or overlap. Knowing what I don't know, I would be pleased if they do.

"*To Plant a Tree*" is also the title of a PBS documentary about a visit to W.S. Merwin at his home in Maui toward the end of his life when his vision was failing, but he was still able to recite large sections of his poems and speak about his ambitions.

About the Author

Robert Harlow is the author of *Places Near and Far* (Louisiana Literature).

www.ingramcontent.com/pod-product-compliance
Lightning Source LLC
LaVergne TN
LVHW010626100826
845148LV00014B/3121

9798901468104